COFFEE
DELIGHTS

PHOTOGRAPHY AND DESIGN
BY KOREN TRYGG
TEXT BY LUCY POSHEK

ANTIOCH GOURMET
GIFT BOOKS

Published by Antioch Publishing Company
Yellow Springs, Ohio 45387

ISBN 0-89954-832-6

COFFEE DELIGHTS

Printed and bound in the U.S.A.

Contents

COFFEE THROUGH TIME

Legend has it that the first *coffea arabica* tree was discovered by a ninth-century Ethiopian shepherd named Kaldi. Noting that his goats were wildly rambunctious after they ate the berries from an unfamiliar tree, Kaldi sampled a few. Before long, everyone in Ethiopia was chewing coffee berries.

It was not until four hundred years later that someone finally thought to roast the beans inside the berries and make a hot drink from them. To a Moslem world that forbade the use of spirits, coffee was a welcome alternative. The Arabs called it *qahwah*, meaning "stimulating wine."

By the fifteenth century Arabia was cultivating coffee trees in Yemen and exporting them across the Levant, from Aden to Cairo to Constantinople. Western travelers to the Levant began returning with reports of an exotic "black water" that had arousing medicinal powers. But the Arabs kept a tight monopoly on the coffee trade until the seventeenth century.

When Venetian traders brought the first coffee beans into Europe during the early 1600's, the drink won instant favor. As coffee perked its way across Europe, the first public coffeehouses, or cafés, opened in Venice,

Marseilles, Oxford, London, and Paris. The coffeehouses served as centers of social and literary life. Such celebrated coffeephiles as Voltaire, Rousseau, Balzac, Flaubert, Hugo, and Benjamin Franklin were frequent *habitués* of the cafés. By the year 1700, there were already two thousand coffeehouses in London alone.

Fearing that the coffeehouses were brewing vice and subversion, several rulers made unsuccessful efforts to suppress them. Charles II tried to close down the coffeehouses in England, but was met with fiery protest. Frederick the Great of Germany prohibited all coffee roasting and even went so far as to hire "coffee smellers" who sniffed outside homes in search of illicit roasters. However, angry demonstrators forced Frederick to relent.

Meanwhile, Dutch traders smuggled some forbidden seedlings out of Arabia and established their own coffee plantations in Ceylon and Java. Over the eighteenth century, other European nations followed suit and began cultivating coffee in their distant colonies. And, after surviving much intrigue during its harrowing voyage from France, the first seedling brought to Martinique eventually propagated most of the coffee in the tropical Americas.

Coffee was brought to America with the European immigrants. Notoriously high tea taxes in the colonies further prompted the switch to coffee. Today, Americans consume about one-third of the world's coffee supply, averaging twenty-six pounds per person yearly.

DELIGHTING IN COFFEE

It is a paradox that coffee is physically stimulating, yet the act of drinking it is considered restful. Whether we luxuriate for hours in a café or take five minutes out from work, the word "coffee" has become synonymous with "break."

In Europe, where the art of leisurely coffee-drinking is carried to its most splendid extreme, it is perfectly

acceptable to sit all afternoon at a sidewalk café with a tiny *demitasse* and newspaper, neither disturbed nor rushed by waiters.

It is a custom which many Americans, in their hurried world of "take-out" coffee, find time-consuming and indulgent. But it is this very act of slowing down that, once experienced, makes the art of coffee-drinking an unmatched pleasure.

The European coffeehouse is an institution steeped in history and tradition. These were the first public places where artists, writers, musicians, politicians, and students could gather to share their ideas. The intellectual fires they stirred played an enormous role in the cultural and political movements of early Europe.

As testimony to their endurance, many of those original coffeehouses are still operating today. The Café Procope, for example, was the first luxurious and truly French coffeehouse to open in Paris in 1683. Venetian violinists still serenade tables at the Café Florian on the Piazza San Marco just as they did in 1720.

There are few more memorable experiences in the world than taking time with a frothy *café au lait* while watching the fashionable Parisian world pass by; or lingering over a mouth-watering strudel and *melange* in an elegant Viennese *kaffeehaus*, surrounded by a glorious sense of history.

But, moreover, it is the luxury of tranquil enjoyment that makes these places so special. All of the senses become sharpened when we slow down and savor our

surroundings; when we take time to appreciate the fragrant aroma of a freshly-made cup of coffee and the nostalgic memories it conjures up; the subtle flavor differences that result from the countless varieties of beans, roasts, and brewing methods; that first inevitably bitter yet comforting taste; the way the liquid mellows with each sip, warms the body and stirs the mind. This is a pleasure we can enjoy no matter where we are in the world or what time of day it is…all in a simple cup of coffee.

A PERFECT CUP OF COFFEE

Making coffee with a degree of ritual often enhances our enjoyment of it. Rather than treating it as a daily chore, look for ways to turn the process into a fun little ceremony. Find a coffee maker and grinder that you truly like using. Buy several blends of beans to satisfy your changing moods during the day. Pick out a favorite cup and claim it for yourself. Try out different flavorings. Take a moment to really taste what you're drinking.

Also remember:

—Buy small quantities of freshly roasted beans and use them fast, as their flavor begins to fade within one month after roasting.

—Grind your beans just before brewing. Whole beans stay fresh longer than ground coffee, which loses its aroma within a week.

—Use the right grind setting. *Extra fine* grinds look powdery and are used for Turkish coffee; *very fine* grinds are for larger espresso machines; *fine* or *drip* grinds are used for small espresso machines, filters, and drip pots; *medium* or *coarse* grinds are best for plunger pots and perked coffees.

—Use fresh (preferably chemical-free), cold water and unbleached filters.

—Of the standard brewing methods, filter and drip have the best results. The plunger pot is also popular, though somewhat messy to clean. Perking and boiling have the least desirable results.

—Measure the coffee and water carefully. Although coffee strength is always a matter of personal choice, a standard measure for the drip method is: 2 level tbsp. (1½ Br. tbsp.) coffee to every ¾ cup (6 fl. oz.) of water.

—For a weaker brew, make regular strength coffee and dilute it with water rather than using fewer grounds.

—If adding milk, heat it first; even better—heat it and whisk it briefly to a froth.

—If the flavor needs some perking up:

• Add a touch of cinnamon, brown sugar, or cocoa powder to the ground beans before brewing.
• Stir the cup with a cinnamon stick.
• Add a splash of vanilla to the pot.
• Garnish the cup with grated lemon or orange peel.
• Throw a cardamom seed or whole clove into the cup.

—Coffee will lose its aroma and become bitter if allowed to sit on a warmer for more than a half-hour.

—Clean the coffee maker and grinder regularly, as residual oils turn rancid quickly.

—Store coffee in an air-tight container. Since coffee easily absorbs refrigerator and freezer odors, room temperature is preferable.

Settlers and cowboys of the American West often roasted their coffee over the campfire. A handful of grounds per cowpoke was thrown in a five-gallon pail of boiling water.

FAVORITE BEANS AND BLENDS

Although restricted to the semi-tropical belt between the tropic of Cancer and the tropic of Capricorn, coffee trees can grow in various climates, soils and altitudes. The exact estate, processing methods, species and age of the coffee are some other factors that account for the wide differences in beans.

Two main species of coffee plants are grown commercially. *Coffea arabica*, the best quality bean, is cultivated in Brazil, Colombia, Arabia, Ethiopia, Indonesia and India. Coffee sold and labelled as an arabica must contain only that particular variety.

Coffea robusta is grown mostly in Africa—the Ivory Coast, Angola and Zaire. A hardier plant, the robusta is so named because it needs less care and lower altitudes. Of inferior quality, robustas are much cheaper than arabicas and widely used in instant coffees and commercial blends.

The roasting process, an art form among the best roasters, largely determines how the coffee will taste. *Light* or *Cinnamon* roasts are used on milder beans such as Colombia and Brazil. *Medium* or *American* roasts are popular in the U.S. and go well with milk. *Full*, *Dark* or *Continental* roasts are traditionally favored in Europe. *Double* or *high roasts* are almost black, with a strong

bitter taste. *French, Italian* and *Espresso* roasts are the darkest, best drunk black.

Even the most expensive coffee beans usually taste better blended than used alone. Often as many as eight complementary coffees are blended together for commercial use. You may like to create your own blend. A mixture of light and dark roasts or mild and sharp beans is an easy way to begin.

It is helpful to know the basic characteristics of beans from the major coffee-producing countries. Here are only a few of the many high-quality brands from around the world:

Brazil - Brazilian beans are usually used as bulk for commercial blends because of their neutral flavor. Santos is regarded as one of the best.

Colombia - Well-balanced acidity, body and sweet taste. Blends well with other coffees. Supremo is the finest grade. Medellín, Manizale, Bogotá, and Armenia are the best regions.

Costa Rica - Full-bodied, nutty flavor, very fragrant aroma. Versatile blender. Alujuela, Heredia and Tarrazu are the finest.

Dominican Republic - Heavy body and strong flavor. Used often in French roasts. Ocoa and Barahona are the better beans.

Ethiopia - Mocha Harrar has an exotic flavor and rich aroma. Longberry Harrar resembles Mocha from Yemen. (In fact, the Mocha beans from Yemen originated in Ethiopia.)

Guatemala - A rising star among coffee connoisseurs. Complex, fruity flavor with spicy overtones and medium body. Cobán, Huehuetenango, and Antiqua are the finest.

Jamaica - The best of the West Indies. Blue Mountain is popular but very expensive and limited in supply.

Java, Indonesia - Among the world's finest and oldest beans. Rich, creamy flavor; spicy, smoky fragrance; and a thick body. Often mixed with Mocha from Yemen.

Kenya - Some of the best coffee in Africa, popular for its dense body and sharp, floral flavor. A good blender with mild coffees.

Kona - Light body, with a mellow, slightly nutty flavor and aroma. Increasingly more expensive as production is on the decline. Usually blended with other beans.

Mexico - Mild acidity, light body, fragrant aroma. The best beans have a hint of hazelnut flavor. Good alone or as blenders.

Sumatra, Indonesia - Smooth and full-bodied, with an intense, earthy flavor. Mandheling is one of the finest.

Venezuela - Mild, delicate, with an evocative aroma. Usually used for blending. Méridas and Caracas are prized beans.

Yemen - Mocha has been treasured throughout history as the most distinctive coffee in the world. Beautifully balanced—smooth, creamy and rich, with a mysterious earthy-chocolate aftertaste. Excellent by itself or blended with Java.

ESPRESSO AND CAPPUCCINO

Whether espresso is made on a little home-brewing Moka pot or a big, elaborate machine, the process is the same: Steaming water is forced through the coffee grounds, which literally presses out the coffee. A slight bitterness results from the higher level of extraction.

No one kind of bean or roast is necessary for espresso, but a low-acid medium to dark roast is favored. In Italy, robusta beans are usually used because they have body and low acid, but their flavor rates low next to arabica beans. A more important factor with espresso is getting a fine grind. If it is too coarse, the result will be watery and sour; too fine results in a bitter, sour drink.

The amount of espresso used is also significant: Try a measurement of slightly less than 2 tbsp. (1½ Br. tbsp.) to every ¼ cup (2 fl. oz.) of water.

The best espressos have a top layer of beige-colored *crema*, or foam—not foam from milk, but from the espresso itself—which is a sign that the water has come through correctly, hot and fast. This can only be achieved with piston or pump machines. The flavor should be slightly bitter at first, but with a sweet, chocolaty aftertaste.

The big, elaborate machines are designed to produce only one tiny cup at a time. It is best not to attempt more than that or the espresso will be overextracted and weak. The stovetop *mokas* are made to produce a greater quantity at a time, but will result in a slightly weaker brew.

Other tips: Preheat the filter holder by running hot water through it empty. And do not compact the ground coffee too tightly or the water cannot come through. Gently level the grounds with a cup or juice glass that has a flat bottom.

In Italy, espresso is served black in a *demitasse*, the traditional small after-dinner cup. In the U.S., a strip of lemon peel is often added to the rim of the cup.

Cappuccino—named after the pale brown color of the robes of Capuchin monks—is made in so many different ways nowadays, it is difficult to know what to expect when ordering it.

The original European version of cappuccino consists of half espresso with half steamed milk, or one-third coffee to two-thirds hot milk, with a generous cap of foam either way. *Caffè macchiato* is "stained" with two teaspoons of foam poured onto the surface; *Caffè latte* is mostly hot milk and no foam.

The American version of cappuccino often includes chocolate with the espresso and steamed milk (or chocolate steamed milk), and sometimes alcohol, with a pinch of powdered chocolate or cinnamon sprinkled on top of the foam.

There is an art to properly steaming milk for cappuccino. Ideally, it should be a smooth head of white foam—neither too bubbly nor too dry.

To steam milk: Start with very fresh, cold milk. Use a cold stainless steel pitcher and fill it no more than half full with milk. Spend a few moments warming the milk up with the steam nozzle of the espresso maker, and then lower the container so that the nozzle hovers just under the surface of the milk. (You should hear a static-like sound.) If foam does not develop soon, warm the milk further and try again. As soon as the foam appears, slowly begin lowering the container and pull the foam up. You should actually be able to feel a slight pull on the container. This "feel" is the key.

"A cup of coffee—real coffee—home-browned, home-ground, home made, that comes to you dark as a hazel-eye, but changes to a golden bronze as you temper it with cream that never cheated, but was real cream from its birth, thick, tenderly yellow, perfectly sweet, neither lumpy nor frothing on the Java: such a cup of coffee is a match for twenty blue devils and will exorcise them all."

HENRY WARD BEECHER

Mexican Cappuccino

*Have ready 1½ cups (12 fl. oz.) hot, strong
coffee. Melt 1 ounce unsweetened (plain) chocolate
in top of double boiler over hot water. Stir in 4 tbsp.
(3 Br. tbsp.) sugar, a dash of salt, and 1 cup (8 fl. oz.)
boiling water. Heat for 5 minutes. In a small saucepan heat ½ cup (4 fl. oz.) milk and the same amount
of whipping cream, just to boiling point. Stir milk
mixture and coffee into chocolate mixture. Beat with
a whisk. Stir in 1 tsp. (¾ Br. tsp.) vanilla extract.
Pour into coffee mugs and sprinkle with cinnamon.*

Mint Cream Espresso

*H*ave ready about 6 ounces of hot espresso. Into a heavy, stemmed 8-ounce glass, pour 1 ounce of coffee-flavored liqueur. Place a silver spoon in the glass to keep it from cracking when adding the hot coffee. Pour in enough coffee to fill the glass to within 2 inches of the rim. Whip 2 tbsp. (1½ Br. tbsp.) heavy cream with 1 tsp. (¾ Br. tsp.) crème de menthe until cream is almost stiff. Top coffee with flavored cream and sprinkle with shavings of dark chocolate.

Breakfast Cappuccino

*H*ave ready 1 cup (8 fl. oz.) hot espresso and 1 cup (8 fl. oz.) scalded milk. Combine with milk in coffee mugs, one part coffee to one part milk. Sprinkle with ground cinnamon.

Espresso with Amaretto

*H*ave ready about 5 ounces of hot espresso. Pour about 2 ounces of amaretto liqueur into a wine glass. Place a silver spoon in the glass to prevent cracking when hot coffee is added. Add the coffee and a dollop of whipped cream.

Chocolate Cappuccino

In a large coffee mug combine 1 tbsp. (³/₄ Br. tbsp.) instant cocoa mix with ¹/₈ tsp. ground ginger and ¹/₄ tsp. ground cinnamon. Add ³/₄ cup (6 fl. oz.) hot coffee and ³/₄ cup (6 fl. oz.) hot milk; stir well. Sprinkle cinnamon on top.

Cappuccino with Nutmeg

Have ready equal amounts of hot espresso and hot milk. Pour equal parts coffee and milk simultaneously into coffee cups. Sprinkle each serving with ground nutmeg.

Espresso with Ice Cream

*B*rew 2 cups (16 fl. oz.) espresso. Put crushed ice into 2 tall glasses; pour 1 cup (8 fl. oz.) of hot espresso into each. Add a scoop of vanilla ice cream to each; serve immediately.

Iced Cappuccino

*B*rew 2 cups (16 fl. oz.) espresso. Chill to room temperature. Blend espresso with 2 cups (16 fl. oz.) whole milk, 4 tbsp. (3 Br. tbsp.) sugar, and ¼ tsp. cinnamon in a blender. Serve in chilled glasses over ice cubes (with no more than 3 cubes per glass).

VIENNESE COFFEE

The first coffeehouse opened in Vienna in the late 1600's when the Turks left five hundred sacks of green coffee beans behind while abandoning their siege of the city. Since then, the Viennese *kaffeehaus* has acquired an unrivaled reputation, continuing in the same *grand epoch* spirit today.

Besides their mouth-watering, multi-layered tortes and *apfelstrudels*, the greatest contribution the Viennese made to coffee drinking was the addition of milk. By now, there are many variations of Viennese coffee: a *Melange*

(half hot milk, half coffee—called *café au lait* in France), a *Brauner* (coffee with just a little milk) or an *Einspänner* (coffee with whipped cream). There is also the *Eiskaffee* (cold black coffee, vanilla ice cream and whipped cream). The American version of Viennese coffee is called *Café Borgia*.

Café Borgia

Melt semisweet (or milk) chocolate—one square or less—in a saucepan with one tbsp. ($^{3}/_{4}$ Br. tbsp.) of cream. Adding one cup of coffee a little at a time, beat with a whisk until frothy. Serve with whipped cream and a sprinkle of ground cinnamon, cocoa or grated orange peel. Another variation: Brew the coffee with a cinnamon stick.

TURKISH COFFEE

Constantinople was one of the first cities to enjoy coffee in a big way. By the mid-sixteenth century, there were already hundreds of coffeehouses in the Turkish city. The houses of the wealthy contained a special room devoted solely to the drinking

of coffee. The serving of *kahveh* was a daily ritual with many rules of etiquette. It became such an institution that Turkish laws permitted women to divorce their husbands for failing to provide the family with coffee.

Made from coffee ground so fine it is almost a powder, Turkish coffee is highly concentrated and usually sweetened (as opposed to Arab coffee, which is unsweetened). It is prepared in small, long-handled copper or brass pots called *ibriks* and served in tiny cups or glasses.

To make a cup of Turkish coffee: Bring one tsp. (¾ Br. tsp.) sugar and ⅔ cup water (5 ⅓ fl. oz.) to a boil, then remove from the fire. Stir in one heaping tbsp. (¾ Br. tbsp.) Turkish ground coffee. Heat again to the point of boiling until the coffee froths up just to the rim.

Repeat this two more times. Before serving, pour a few drops of cold water into the *ibrik* or simply rap the pot to settle the grounds. Be sure that some of the creamy froth is shaken into the cup. Since some coffee grounds will escape into the cup, allow the coffee to stand for a few minutes before drinking it. You may wish to add a cardamom seed, cinnamon, nutmeg or cloves to the brew.

In Turkey and the Arab countries, where coffee is a symbol of hospitality, it is customary to pound the roasted beans by hand with a mortar and pestle. The most important guests are served first. Each cup must have its share of foam—accomplished with a slight shaking of the hand as it is poured—and be filled at least half full, but not too full, or it is considered an insult. The guest is expected to drink at least two cups but no more than three (another breach of etiquette). Coffee is sometimes served with *friandises*—assorted sweetmeats such as dates in syrup and crystallized orange peels.

In early Greece, a girl could politely reject her suitor simply by serving his Turkish coffee without any foam.

Madame de Pompadour, mistress of Louis XV, liked to drink her coffee in an exotic Arabian setting—served by a Nubian maid while reclined amidst luxurious silk pillows.

ICED COFFEE

The key to making good iced coffee is to first brew good hot coffee, and no more than three hours in advance. Cover the coffee to preserve the aroma and allow it to come to room temperature. Then chill it in the refrigerator.

If using ice cubes, prepare either double-strength coffee or coffee ice cubes so that the coffee will not be too diluted.

Flavorings for iced coffee are much the same as for hot coffee (with the exception of ice cream, of course)—lemon twists, rum, chocolate, cinnamon, honey…and even vodka, as you will see.

It is said that iced coffee was invented by the French colonial armies while stationed in blistering North Africa.

Mocha Float

Brew a light-roast coffee and chill. Fill a large coffee cup or mug with the chilled coffee, then add a large scoop of chocolate ice cream. Top with whipped cream and sprinkle with cocoa powder.

Frozen Coffee

Dissolve ¼ cup (2 fl. oz.) sugar in 2 cups (16 fl. oz.) hot, freshly brewed extra-strength coffee. Add 2 tsp. (1½ Br. tsp.) vanilla. Pour mixture into an 8-inch square pan. Freeze until almost firm (30 to 60 minutes). Meanwhile grate an ounce of semisweet (or milk) chocolate. Break up the frozen coffee with a fork and stir in the chocolate. Return mixture to freezer; freeze until firm. Break up mixture with a fork, then spoon into dessert glasses. Top each serving with sweetened whipped cream. Garnish with chocolate-covered coffee beans.

Orange & Spice Coffee

Brew 4 cups (32 fl. oz.) extra-strength coffee. Place 10 whole cloves and 4 large strips of orange peel in a large teapot or heat-proof pitcher. Pour the hot coffee into the teapot. Let mixture steep for an hour, then chill it in the refrigerator in a covered container. Strain and serve over ice.

Iced Café au Lait

Brew a cup of double-strength coffee. Chill. Combine with 2 tbsp. (1½ Br. tbsp.) confectioners' (icing) sugar, 1 cup (8 fl. oz.) whole milk, and 3 cups (24 fl. oz.) chopped ice in a blender. Blend until creamy.

Moose Milk

Place ½ cup (4 fl. oz.) coffee, ⅓ cup (2 ⅔ fl. oz.) vodka, and ¼ cup (2 fl. oz.) crème de cacao in a blender. Fill blender halfway to the top with vanilla ice cream and ice cubes. Blend mixture together.

LACED COFFEE

There is perhaps nothing so satisfying after dinner as a rich, spirit-laced coffee. Called a *cordial* in France and a *corretto* in Italy, good laced coffees do not require an expensive brand of liquor. Cognac, Armagnac and Grand Marnier are, of course, luxurious complements to hot coffee, but they are even better served on the side. (This combination is also said to aid digestion.)

Other spirits that go well in coffee are crème de menthe, ouzo, Frangelico, Cointreau, crème de cacao, curaçao and Benedictine. The sugar-cane flavor of rum and the smoky taste of whiskey have both been long-time favorites in coffee.

Coffee-flavored liqueurs make natural complements to coffee. Kahlúa, from Mexico, and the slightly lighter Tia Maria, from Jamaica, are the two best known coffee liqueurs. They also provide sweet mixers for such drinks as Black and White Russians.

To make laced coffee: Fill a cup or heat-proof glass three-quarters full of strong, hot, black coffee. Sweeten if desired and add a jigger of your favorite spirit. You may also top with whipped cream.

Orange Mocha Coffee

In a small mixing bowl combine 2 cups (16 fl. oz.) strong, hot coffee with ½ cup (4 fl. oz.) orange liqueur and ½ cup (4 fl. oz.) chocolate syrup. Mix well and pour in coffee cups. Serve with whipped cream.

Irish Coffee

Place a sugar cube or one tsp. (¾ Br. tsp.) sugar in the bottom of an Irish coffee glass. Pour hot coffee over the sugar, filling to within a half-inch of the top. Stir until dissolved. Add 1½ ounces Irish whiskey and top with whipped cream.

Café Brûlot

*H*ave ready a heat-proof serving bowl. Brew 3 cups (24 fl. oz.) coffee to double strength. In a small saucepan over medium heat, heat the following ingredients: 1 cup (8 fl. oz.) brandy, 1 tsp. (³/₄ Br. tsp.) grated orange peel, ½ tsp. grated lemon peel, 3 tbsp. (2½ Br. tbsp.) sugar, 6 whole cloves, 4 whole allspice, 1 cinnamon stick, and 1 tsp. (³/₄ Br. tsp.) vanilla extract. When brandy is hot, pour mixture into heat-proof serving bowl. Carefully ignite brandy and let burn for 60 seconds. Slowly pour hot coffee into flaming brandy. Stir mixture and ladle into demitasse cups. Serve without cream or any added sugar.

Keoki Coffee

*P*our a ³/₄-ounce shot of brandy and a ³/₄-ounce shot of Kahlúa into a cup of hot coffee. Top with whipped cream.

Danish Coffee

*I*n a very large, heavy saucepan combine the following: 8 cups (64 fl. oz.) hot coffee, 1 cup (8 fl. oz.) rum, ³/₄ cup (6 fl. oz.) sugar, 2 cinnamon sticks, and 12 whole cloves. Cover and keep on low heat for about 2 hours. Serve in coffee mugs.

A WORD ABOUT CAFFEINE

Coffee affects everyone differently, and although it has not been proven that caffeinated coffee is harmful when drunk in moderation, a full twenty percent of coffee-drinkers in the U.S. have switched to decaf.

Decaffeination processes are steadily improving to the point where the loss in flavor over caffeinated beans is sometimes imperceptible. The catch, however, is that most commercial decafs rely on the least-flavorful robusta beans. Also, the chemicals found in some decaf beans have recently been questioned for their adverse effects on cholesterol levels.

A few suggestions for the caffeine-sensitive:

—Darker roasting reduces the amount of caffeine in coffee. This means that rich French and Italian roasts are usually less powerful, caffeine-wise, than a weak American brew.

—Arabica-bean coffees—found in the better quality brands—contain half the caffeine of robusta beans. Instant coffees, consisting of mostly robusta beans, pack the strongest punch.

—Adding milk or cream to coffee seems to lessen the stimulating effects of caffeine. Drinking coffee on a full stomach—during or after a meal—works similarly.

Coffee-Flavored Desserts

Cappuccino Marble Cheesecake

1½ cups (12 fl. oz.) graham cracker
   (digestive biscuit) crumbs
¼ cup (2 fl. oz.) sugar
6 tbsp. (4½ Br. tbsp.) melted butter
4 8-ounce pkgs. cream cheese, softened
2 tsp. (1½ Br. tsp.) vanilla
1¾ cups (14 fl. oz.) sugar
6 eggs
2 cups (16 fl. oz.) light cream
2 ounces unsweetened (plain) chocolate
6 tbsp. (4½ Br. tbsp.) strong black coffee
2 tbsp. (1½ Br. tbsp.) finely ground coffee

*Melt chocolate with coffee and coffee grounds
in a double boiler, stirring until smooth. Let mixture
cool.*

*Combine crumbs, sugar and butter. Press in bottom
and 2 inches up sides of a 9-inch springform (loose
bottom) pan. Set aside.*

*Beat cream cheese and vanilla until fluffy. Gradu-
ally beat in sugar. Add eggs, one at a time, beating*

just until blended. Stir in cream. Combine 3 cups of the batter with cooled chocolate. Pour plain cheese mixture into crust. Gradually add chocolate mixture, using zig-zag motion.

Bake at 450°F for 15 minutes, then reduce heat to 300°F. Continue baking for 1 hour or until cheesecake begins to crack at edges and knife inserted halfway in center comes out clean. Turn off oven. Cool cheesecake in oven with door ajar for 1 hour. Chill thoroughly, ideally overnight. Remove sides of pan before serving. Top with whipped cream around edges and chocolate-coated coffee beans or dusting of cocoa powder, if desired. Serves 10.

Espresso Tiramisu

16 ladyfingers
½ cup (4 fl. oz.) espresso or strong black coffee
1 tbsp. (¾ Br. tbsp.) brandy or amaretto
5 eggs, separated
1½ cups (12 fl. oz.) powdered (icing) sugar
8 ounces mascarpone cheese, softened
2 tbsp. (1½ Br. tbsp.) unsweetened cocoa

Cream egg yolks and powdered sugar with electric mixer until smooth. Add mascarpone and beat until smooth. In separate bowl, whip egg whites until stiff.

Stir a quarter of the whites into mascarpone mixture to lighten. Quickly fold in remaining whites.

Arrange ladyfingers on bottom of a rectangular or oval serving dish. Pour coffee and liquor over ladyfingers. Then pour mascarpone mixture over ladyfingers. Sift cocoa over the top and refrigerate, covered, 1 to 2 hours. Serves 6 to 8.

(Cream cheese may be substituted for the mascarpone if necessary.)

Java Truffles

6 ounces semisweet (or milk) chocolate, cut into pieces
2 tbsp. (1½ Br. tbsp.) strong black coffee
2 tbsp. (1½ Br. tbsp.) cream
1½ tbsp. (1 Br. tbsp.) coffee-flavored liqueur
2 tbsp. (1½ Br. tbsp.) unsweetened cocoa powder

Melt chocolate, coffee and cream in a double boiler over hot water. Stir well. Pour mixture into bowl and beat with an electric mixer for 10 minutes until thick. Add liqueur and beat 2-3 minutes longer. Cover and chill.

Shape chocolate into ½-inch balls. Roll in cocoa powder until evenly coated. Refrigerate or freeze until ready to serve.

Gray's Mocha Cake

3 squares (3 oz.) unsweetened (plain) chocolate
½ cup (4 fl. oz.) strong black coffee or espresso
⅔ cup (5⅓ fl. oz.) firmly packed dark brown sugar
5 tbsp. (3¾ Br. tbsp.) butter, softened
⅔ cup (5⅓ fl. oz.) granulated sugar
2 eggs
1½ cups (12 fl. oz.) white flour, sifted
1½ tsp. (1⅛ Br. tsp.) baking powder
½ tsp. baking soda
¼ tsp. salt
⅔ cup (5⅓ fl. oz.) milk
2 tbsp. (1½ Br. tbsp.) coffee-flavored liqueur

Grease two 8-inch cake pans and dust with flour. Preheat oven to 350°F.

In the top of a double boiler, over hot, not boiling, water, melt the chocolate with the coffee and brown sugar. Cool and add liqueur.

With an electric mixer, combine the butter and granulated sugar, beating until light. Beat in eggs, then the chocolate mixture. Add dry ingredients to the batter gradually, alternating with milk, until batter is smooth.

Pour batter into cake pans and bake on middle rack for 15-20 minutes, until a toothpick comes out clean. Remove from oven and cool before removing from pans.

Mocha Icing

1 square (1 oz.) semisweet (or milk) chocolate
2 tbsp. (1 ½ Br. tbsp.) strong black coffee
1 tbsp. (¾ Br. tbsp.) coffee-flavored liqueur
3 tbsp. (2 ¼ Br. tbsp.) butter
1 ½ cups (12 fl. oz.) powdered (icing) sugar, sifted

In the top of a double boiler, melt the chocolate with the coffee, stirring frequently, never allowing the water underneath to boil. Cool, then add liqueur and powdered sugar, whipping until smooth. Spread over both cake layers. Can garnish with a light colored coffee-butter-sugar icing (omitting the liqueur and chocolate) and top with coffee beans.

"Hardly have I drunk coffee when everything falls into place. Thoughts come flooding like battalions of a great army on the battlefield."

HONORÉ DE BALZAC
(who drank 20-30 cups of coffee a day)

Coffee has two virtues, it is wet and warm.

DUTCH PROVERB

Shown clockwise from the left:
Gray's Mocha Cake,
Café Mousse, and Java Truffles

Café Mousse

4 tbsp. (3 Br. tbsp.) ground coffee
½ cup (4 fl. oz.) water
6 ounces unsweetened (plain) chocolate, cut into pieces
6 tbsp. (4 ½ Br. tbsp.) butter, cut into pieces
4 eggs, separated
¾ cup (6 fl. oz.) granulated sugar
3 tbsp. (2 ¼ Br. tbsp.) coffee-flavored liqueur
½ cup (4 fl. oz.) cream, beaten until thick
½ tsp. salt

Prepare 4 to 24 hours in advance.

Make a concentrated coffee by bringing the water to a boil with the coffee and allowing it to infuse. Strain and set aside. Melt chocolate with coffee in double boiler over hot, not boiling, water. Then add butter, bit by bit, beating with a wire whisk until smooth. Cool.

In a mixing bowl, beat egg yolks and sugar with an electric beater until creamy. Add chocolate mixture, continuing to beat. Then beat in liqueur.

In separate bowl, beat cream until thick and fold in carefully. Beat egg whites and salt until stiff, and fold in last.

Pour mousse into serving bowl or small soufflé dishes. Chill thoroughly. Serves 10-12.

*"Coffee should be black as the Devil,
hot as Hell, pure as an angel, sweet as love."*

PRINCE TALLEYRAND

GRAPHIC DESIGN BY GRETCHEN GOLDIE

FRONT COVER STYLED BY SUE TALLON

PHOTO ASSISTANCE BY SUSAN MALJAN

ACKNOWLEDGMENTS

MICHAELEEN CRAWFORD, MARY HAFT,
DICK HEALY, DEBORAH JOYCE, EMILY MEIERDING,
LINDA TRYGG, MARY ULASAK